JOHN PAUL II

The Pope Who Modernised the Catholic Church

Written by Benoît-J. Pédretti
In collaboration with Pierre Frankignoulle
Translated by Rebecca Neal

History 50MINUTES.com

JOHN PAUL II

KEY INFORMATION

- **Born:** 18 May 1920 in Wadowice (Poland).
- **Died:** 2 April 2005 in Vatican City.
- **Pontificate:** 1978-2005.
- **Canonisation:** 27 April 2014.
- **Main achievements:**
    - The modernisation of the Catholic Church and the implementation of the reforms of the Second Vatican Council.
    - Major political influence during the fall of communist regimes in Eastern Europe in 1989.
    - The development of a close relationship with Catholics across the world, with visits to 129 countries.
    - The promotion of a social doctrine in favour of the defence of human rights and the fight against poverty.

INTRODUCTION

"Do not be afraid. Open wide the doors for Christ. To his saving power open the boundaries of States, economic and political systems, the vast fields of culture, civilization and development" (*Homily for the Inauguration of the Pontificate of John Paul II*). John Paul II began his time as pope with this call for hope on 22 October 1978. His election as pope of the Catholic Church came as a great surprise to everyone, and in many respects he was a very unusual choice. He was the first non-Italian cardinal to take on the role for over four centuries, and came from the other side of the Iron Curtain.

His native Poland had a deep-rooted Catholic tradition, but had fallen under the control of communism in 1944.

He soon made his mark on the position, effecting a major renewal of the role of pope. As a man of the Church, he was committed to promoting Christian identity, delivering a message of tolerance to as many people as possible, and rekindling interreligious dialogue. As a head of state, he employed his talent on the world diplomatic stage in order to persuade and sway totalitarian regimes, with a skill and energy that undoubtedly mark him out as one of the greatest popes of the 20th century.

THE LIFE OF JOHN PAUL II

A LATE VOCATION

Karol Józef Wojtyła was born on 18 May 1920 in Wadowice, a small town in the Eastern European region of Galicia, near Krakow in the south of Poland. As a teenager, he had a passion for the theatre and wrote several plays, and he understood the dramatic power of speech from a very early age. Although he initially wanted to become an actor, he ended up enrolling at the Jagiellonian University to study humanities, specialising in Polish philosophy. When the universities were closed due to the Nazi occupation in 1939, he put on plays in secret, which he saw as a means of resistance. When he was forced to work in the Zakrzówek stone quarry, and then the Solway chemical factory in Krakow, he learnt about the hard manual work of labourers.

He decided to embark on an ecclesiastical career in 1942. He was first accepted into the clandestine seminary run by Prince Adam Sapieha (1876-1951), cardinal archbishop of Krakow, before becoming acquainted with spirituality and studying the works of Saint Louis-Marie Grignion de Montfort (French priest canonised in 1947, 1673-1716). He was ordained a priest on 1 November 1946. He continued his theological training at the *Angelicum*, the Dominican university in Rome, where he learnt French and Spanish before defending his thesis, entitled *The Doctrine of Faith in St. John of the Cross*. At this time, he travelled to France and Belgium, where he discovered and was won over by new, modern forms of evangelisation.

When he returned to Poland in June 1948, he was appointed priest in the village of Niegowić, then in the university parish of Saint Florian in Krakow, where he implemented a range of activities aimed at young people. He also taught at the university and, in 1953, wrote a philosophy thesis entitled *Re-evaluation of the possibility of founding a Catholic ethic on the ethical system of Max Scheler* (German philosopher, 1874-1928). In a Poland which was now communist, he criticised the Marxist ideology of Stalin (Soviet leader, 1878-1953), although he did not take a public stand.

A SOCIALLY COMMITTED BISHOP AND AN ACTIVIST CARDINAL

Karol Wojtyła was ordained as bishop on 28 September 1958 by Pope Pius XII (1876-1958) and, among other responsibilities, was tasked with the pastoral care of students as an auxiliary bishop to the archbishop of Krakow. At the age of 38, he was at the time the youngest bishop in Poland. Without being a fanatical activist, he enthusiastically took on the task of defending the Catholic Church, which had been persecuted by the authoritarian regime of the Polish People's Republic, by supporting the construction of a church in Nowa Huta, a working-class district of Krakow which did not have its own place of worship.

During the Second Vatican Council (1962-1965), he took part in the debate on the modernisation of the Church by supporting the role of lay figures and ecumenical dialogue (which encourages unity among all the Christian Churches) as the natural spokesman of the Polish bishops. He caught the eye of Pope Paul VI (1897-1978) and was appointed Archbishop of Krakow on 30 December 1963, before becoming the youngest cardinal of the Catholic Church on 26 June 1967, at the age of 47. He then demonstrated strong conviction in his defence of students, the Jewish community and labourers, who had all been persecuted by the communist regime. He emphasised human rights and enthusiastically preached in Rome in 1976, where he attracted the attention of his fellow cardinals.

After the sudden death of Pope Paul VI in 1978, John Paul I (1912-1978) was elected pope, but died after just 33 days in the role. Another conclave was then called. After eight rounds of voting, and to many people's surprise, Karol Wojtyła was elected pope of the Catholic Church on 16 October 1978, at the age of 58. He took the name of John Paul II.

AN UNUSUAL POPE

As the first pope from a Slavic country in the history of Catholicism and the first non-Italian pope since 1523, John Paul II was out of the ordinary in all respects. He wanted to ensure close contact with Catholics by going out to meet the faithful, which increased the visibility of the role. To do this, he left Rome and even Italy. In the course of 104 journeys to the four corners of the world, he was seen by over 500 million followers of the Church.

He was a passionate defender of human dignity and democracy, and denounced poverty and all forms of oppression. He met Mother Teresa (1910-1997), whom he greatly admired, on a number of occasions. In the course of his several visits to countries in Central and South America, he strongly opposed totalitarian regimes. Thanks to his non-dogmatic open-mindedness, he was able to significantly improve interreligious dialogue. He laid the cornerstone for this dialogue by inviting 194 religious leaders from all the world's major religions to a universal prayer service for world peace at Assisi in 1986. Later that year, he established World Youth Day, with the aim of delivering a religious message to the youngest believers. Nonetheless, some of his unwavering stances on abortion, contraception and the celibacy of priests led to sometimes fierce controversies.

John Paul II was also a head of state (albeit a microstate) with real international political influence. In this capacity, he made a major contribution to the fall of the Iron Curtain through targeted action in Poland alongside Lech Walesa (Polish statesman, born in 1943) and repeated interventions with the Soviet government. In 1990, he opposed the Gulf War and in 1991, during one of his visits to Poland, he denounced the marked excesses of capitalism.

DID YOU KNOW?

During his pontificate, John Paul II took part in 1475 discussions with political figures, 738 of which were with heads of state.

Suffering from Parkinson's disease, he appeared in public less and less frequently from the early 2000s onwards. He died on 2 April 2005 after more than 26 years as pope, making his pontificate the third longest in history.

He was beatified on 1 May 2011 by his successor, Pope

Benedict XVI (born in 1927), then canonised on 27 April 2014 by Pope Francis (born in 1936). He is now one of the saints of the Catholic Church, and his feast day is celebrated on 22 October.

Catholics witness the beatification of John Paul II in Vatican City.

CONTEXT

JOHN PAUL II AND POLAND: FROM NAZI OCCUPATION TO EUROPEAN INTEGRATION

The young Karol Wojtyła received his religious training in a very unusual context, marked by extreme violence, in the heart of Poland, which was first under Nazi occupation, and then under Soviet influence. When he became pope, he would retain a subtle skill for diplomacy.

On 1 September 1939, Poland was invaded by Nazi Germany, triggering the Second World War (1939-1945). In accordance with the secret Nazi-Soviet Pact, the USSR then invaded Poland on 17 September, wiping the country from the map for the fourth time in its history: part of Polish territory was directly annexed to the Third Reich, another part was annexed to the Ukrainian and Belorussian Republics of the USSR, and the central part was controlled by the Nazis, who set up a general government in Krakow. The occupying forces wanted to destroy all forms of resistance by eradicating the Polish elites: intellectuals, including 189 professors from the University of Krakow, which was closed, civil servants and religious figures were imprisoned and deported. Seminaries were outlawed, theatres were closed and newspapers were suspended. The extermination of the Jewish community in Europe was methodically organised from Poland. Around 20 000 Jews, almost a quarter of the population of Krakow, were deported. In January 1945, when the war was approaching its end, the city was liberated by the Red Army and integrated into the new Polish Republic. From then on, the country was under communist influence.

In 1958, the new Bishop of Krakow, Karol Wojtyła, had to position himself in the face of this nascent totalitarian environment. As his statements were initially moderate, the authorities did not consider him a threat to the regime. However, some people criticised his weak stance, and even suggested that he was overly indulgent towards the ruling power. It was only from 1964 onwards, when he became archbishop, that he openly expressed opinions that were hostile to communism. In 1970, then again in 1976, he tried to soften the repression of workers' revolts and the increasing pressure placed on religious authorities. He was then put under surveillance.

His election as pope in 1978 resounded like a thunderclap in the communist world. In June 1979, he returned to his native country, where he enjoyed considerable popularity. He had no qualms about defending freedom of expression and association in full view of the Polish authorities, who were taken by surprise and particularly embarrassed. During the workers' rebellion in Gdansk in 1980, Lech Walesa, founder of the Solidarity trade union movement, had portraits of the new pope hung on the railings of striking shipyards. He thus compelled John Paul II to take a stand, and the pope could not help but pronounce his support for the Polish cause. When Wojciech Jaruzelski (Polish statesman, 1923-2014), who had just been appointed leader of the country, imposed martial law in December 1981, John Paul II tried to restore calm to the country to avoid a bloodbath. He returned to the country in 1983 and reaffirmed his support for opponents of the regime.

John Paul II visiting Poland in 1979.

During the 1980s, he increased his diplomatic activity in opposition to Moscow and became closer to the Reagan (American president, 1911-2004) administration through the profitable exchange of confidential information. In 1992, the Soviet leader Mikhail Gorbachev (born in 1931), aware of the work of John Paul II, stated that "Everything that has happened these last years in Eastern Europe could never have happened without the presence of this Pope, without the major role, including the major political role, that he has played on the world stage" (Dziwisz, 2008: 182). This clearly indicates the importance of the pope's work.

Armed with both moral and political authority, he defended human rights in front of the international community in visionary speeches at the United Nations in 1979 and 1995, and before UNESCO in 1980 and the European Parliament in 1988.

In 1989, after the fall of the Berlin Wall, the Eastern European republics abandoned communism one by one. On 1 January 1990, the Third Polish Republic was proclaimed. The new nation gradually aligned itself more closely with the West, and joined NATO in 1999. Once the spectre of communism had disappeared, John Paul II warned his compatriots against capitalism. Moreover, he advocated gradual but necessary integration in Europe, and Poland became a member of the European Union on 1 May 2004.

JOHN PAUL II'S ACTION ACROSS THE WORLD

A GLOBE-TROTTING SPEAKER

Early on, John Paul II proved to be a very independent thinker. As such, he closely observed the institutional workings and organisation of the Catholic Church in order to develop a personal opinion about of it, without the influence of habits and customs. He then shared his ideas in carefully crafted speeches, which he wrote himself, and did not hesitate to depart from the rigid protocol of the Curia whenever he felt it necessary. He also prioritised direct contact with the faithful and enthusiastically mingled with the crowds until the assassination attempt against him in 1981.

He was convinced of the need for strong communication and of the power of images in a changing society. As such, he held press conferences, which were sometimes unscripted, and even spoke to reporters on planes. He also began giving weekly audiences, where he addressed crowds in St. Peter's Square in Rome. In total, over 18 million Catholics came to Rome while he was pope. He also received anonymous pilgrims and heads of state, who were keen to meet him: in this way, over 1500 people had the privilege of speaking with him personally.

John Paul II visiting New York in 1979.

With the aim of promoting a universal missionary message, he increased the number of Apostolic Nunciatures, which functioned like embassies for the Holy See abroad. By the end of his time as pope, there were 174 papal delegations of this kind, almost one per country. He was a great traveller and set out to meet people himself. These missions, which were sometimes political, sometimes religious and sometimes a mixture of the two, were carefully organised and widely covered in the media. Like Pope Paul VI, John Paul II would kiss the ground when he set foot in a new territory.

DID YOU KNOW?

John Paul II undertook 104 journeys, visited 129 countries and covered over 100 million kilometres, the equivalent of travelling around the world 28 times. He was also the first pope to visit the United Kingdom, Morocco, India and Australia.

JOHN PAUL II AND LATIN AMERICA

The pope visited Latin America several times. For instance, in 1978 he visited Mexico, where he visited the Basilica of Our Lady of Guadalupe. During this visit, he defended the country's indigenous populations and denounced injustices and human rights infringements everywhere he went. In July 1979, during a trip to Nicaragua, he strongly criticised priests who had become ministers under the Sandinista government and, in June 1980, he denounced the political involvement of liberation theologians in Brazil. The liberation theology movement, which emerged in the late 1960s in Latin America, intended to reconcile revolution and Christianity by mobilising the masses against injustice. Although John Paul II supported the fight against poverty, he had no intention of encouraging armed revolutions. He believed that religious believers did not have to overthrow governments, and strongly condemned this quasi-Marxist ideology.

However, when dictatorships attacked the clergy, the pope was quick to react. This was particularly the case after the assassination of the archbishop Oscar Romero in El Salvador in 1980, and in 1987, when he called on Augusto Pinochet (Chilean general and military dictator, 1915-2006) to resign and hand over power to the Chilean people.

A POPE IN FOCUS

Although the pope was exposed wherever he went, and particularly in countries that were sometimes hostile to Catholicism, it was in St. Peter's Square, Rome, with 20 000 people present to hear him speak, that an attempt was made on his life on 13 May 1981. Mehmet Ali Ağca (born in 1958), a 23-year-old Turkish man, shot the pope three times at almost point-blank range with a 9 mm semi-automatic pistol. The pope was wounded and was rushed to the hospital, but the bullets had missed his vital organs and so his life was not in danger.

The world was stunned, and theories about the assassination attempt proliferated: was it an isolated or an ordered attack? Was the gunman a lone wolf, or was the shooting an Islamist plot or a Soviet conspiracy? These questions remain unanswered.

In 1982, the pope was visiting the shrine of the Virgin in Fátima, Portugal, when he was attacked with a bayonet by the Spanish fundamentalist Catholic priest Juan María Fernández y Krohn (born in 1948). The pope's injuries were not serious, and the attack was carefully concealed from the public.

Nonetheless, drastic security measures were put in place: from then on, the pope only travelled around in a raised, armoured car with bulletproof windows, nicknamed the 'popemobile'.

A UNIVERSAL MESSAGE

In 1986, John Paul II, who wanted to transmit a religious message that had universal relevance rather than being limited to the West, established World Youth Day. This day was aimed at young adults in search of their identity, and took the form of periodic meetings, to be held every two to three years. The initiative was an immediate success, and the tenth World Youth Day in Manila, the Philippines (10-15 January 1995) brought together up to 5 million young people around the pope.

At the same time, John Paul II encouraged the expansion of more or less controversial movements, such as the Charismatic Movement and Opus Dei, but also the promulgation of a universal catechism.

THE CATECHISM OF THE CATHOLIC CHURCH

The *Catechism of the Catholic Church* is a work intended for the instruction of the Catholic faithful. It is over 650 pages long, and brings together the main points of Catholic dogmas, spread over four sections based on the model of the Roman Catechism issued after the Council of Trent (1545-1563):

- the Profession of Faith;
- the Celebration of the Christian Mystery;
- Life in Christ;
- Christian Prayer.

After nine successive versions, it was approved in 1991 and published in 35 languages in 1998. John Paul II closely followed its production, and thought of it as an instrument for clearly explaining doctrine, while giving valuable and concrete responses to questions of daily life for Catholics. A more didactic abridged version was published by Benedict XVI in 2005.

For the Jubilee in 2000, the pope invited millions of pilgrims to Rome to celebrate the holy year and the 2000th anniversary of the Church, and to deepen their personal faith, which is at the heart of the international Christian community.

Also at this time, a reconciliation with the great principles of humanity was finally underway. Galileo (Italian mathematician and astronomer, 1564-1642) had been condemned by the Church in 1633 for showing that the Earth orbits around the sun, but in 1992, John Paul II announced that this had been an error. The theory of evolution, first put forward by Charles Darwin (1809-1882), was accepted in 1996, thus putting an end to the age-old disputes between science and religion.

DID YOU KNOW?

John Paul II wrote a great number of religious and secular works:

- 3 plays;
- 14 encyclicals;
- 22 books;

- 42 ecclesiastical letters;
- 20 351 speeches.

MAJOR PROGRESS IN INTERRELIGIOUS DIALOGUE

One of the key motivations behind John Paul II's activities was his desire to bring different religions closer together, without syncretism (the fusion of disparate doctrines). This was shown first of all through an ecumenical dialogue between the Christian religions. The Catholic Church became closer to the Protestant faith, with a joint declaration with the Lutheran Church in 1998, and then to the Orthodox Church during visits to Romania (1999) and Greece (2004). Only the Russian Orthodox Church rejected the pope's olive branch, probably for reasons that were as much political as purely religious, as John Paul II had never been welcomed in the USSR.

An important step was also made towards Judaism, Islam and Buddhism. John Paul II had been in contact with Jewish culture since his childhood and witnessed the deportation of Jews during the Second World War. He recognised the State of Israel in 1993, and from 20 to 26 March 2000 he embarked on a pilgrimage to the Holy Land. He went to Bethlehem, then to Jerusalem to the Yad Vashem memorial and the Western Wall, where he asked for forgiveness for the anti-Semitic acts committed by Christians throughout history. He also carried out a large amount of diplomatic work towards Islam, with visits to Turkey, Morocco and

Tunisia. He became the first pope to set foot in a mosque, when he went to the Great Mosque of Damascus (Syria) in May 2001 to pray to the relics of St. John the Baptist. Finally, he met the Dalai Lama (born in 1935) five times between 1980 and 1990, and the two men developed a bond based on mutual respect and friendship.

John Paul II visiting the Great Mosque of Damascus.

However, the main symbol of this interfaith dialogue, one of the high points of John Paul II's pontificate, remains the meeting in Assisi, which began on 27 October 1986 with a world prayer day. Announced to coincide with the UN's International Year of Peace, it brought together almost 200 religious leaders and representatives to reaffirm their com- mitment to lasting world peace. This day was a resounding success, so similar meetings were held in 1993 and 2002, and under John Paul II's successor in 2011.

> ## DID YOU KNOW?
>
> John Paul II gave a new impetus to the worship of saints by elevating those whose Christian faith was particularly remarkable or heroic to the rank of blessed or saints. As such, during his pontificate there were 1338 beatifications, including that of Mother Teresa in 2003, and 482 canonisations.

OFTEN VISIONARY BUT SOMETIMES RISKY STANCES

In countless addresses, the pope showed himself to be strict with regard to the principles of faith and traditional morality, as was the case in the October 1993 encyclical *Splendor veritatis*, in which he set out the theological and anthropological foundations of morality. His stances were often very personal and widely opposed, even within the Catholic Church.

Some thought that he was moving too quickly. In particular, a small group of traditionalists around the French archbishop Marcel Lefebvre (1905-1991) thought that the Second Vatican Council and the reforms begun by John Paul II were too progressive and went against Church tradition. Lefebvre would later break away from Rome and give his own orders to bishops. The group was excommunicated in 1988.

Conversely, others thought that he did not go far enough in his reforms: indeed, he named the conservative theologian Joseph Ratzinger (born in 1927), the future Benedict XVI, Prefect of the Congregation for the Doctrine of the Faith. Furthermore, certain firm and fiercely defended stances did not mesh with the reality on the ground or the regional context. For example, in 1994 (the International Year of the Family), he re-emphasised the foundations of the theory of sexuality, which only recognised relations between two people within traditional marriage, thus confirming the Church's opposition to sex outside marriage, homosexuality and contraception, which was deemed unnecessary and contrary to natural procreation. His unshakeable opposition to the use of condoms as a method of contraception or a form of protection against sexually transmitted diseases was very strongly criticised given the AIDS epidemic ravaging Africa. Finally, his opposition to abortion, euthanasia and all forms of genetic engineering, all of which he conflated with murder, sparked fierce controversies. Moreover, his beliefs that divorced people should not be allowed to receive the sacraments and that the marriage of priests and the ordination of women should be forbidden were particularly badly received, especially as these practices were often allowed in other Christian denominations. Conversely, in 2001 he requested that the sexual abuse of minors by priests be systematically reported out of concern for transparency.

IMPACT

THE REFORM OF CATHOLICISM

The reforms of the Second Vatican Council were largely accomplished with the introduction of Catholic rites and rituals in the vernacular, meaning that the faithful could finally read and understand them. The principle of religious freedom was reaffirmed, as was the principle of faith as an independent process resulting from an individual's personal awareness rather than the imposition of a collection of rules to follow. Even the Curia, the bloated government body of the Vatican, which was controlled mainly by Italians, was reformed, democratised and renewed. The pope appointed 232 new cardinals from all over the world, as well as 3500 bishops, in order to make the Catholic church unquestionably legitimate and adequately represented across the world. These steps had a number of additional consequences, such as the encouragement of new forms of spirituality or congregations outside the parish or episcopal structures of the traditional Church. Consequently, John Paul II's pontificate saw the development of L'Arche, a community for Christians with disabilities, and the Emmanuel Community, with its roots in the Charismatic Movement, in France, and the Community of Sant'Egido, established to fight poverty, in Italy.

A RENEWAL OF THE RELIGIOUS MESSAGE

The Church now aimed to transmit a universal message, and made major efforts to communicate this through modern channels. The change in the image of the papacy brought it right into the 20th century; the pope was now accessible to everyone. He went from an untouchable icon to a human being who was deeply committed to the fight against inequality and for human rights. He appeared all over the world whenever there was an opportunity for religious intervention, with meticulously organised visits. Above all, these appearances allowed him to reinforce his pro-democracy social doctrine and to denounce poverty and all forms of enslavement of humans.

John Paul II visiting Gabon in 1983.

A new openness to other religions through peaceful dialogue paved the way for the idea of joint action against extremism and for world peace. Moreover, his opposition to liberation theology was based on the fundamental principle of a non-violent religion, which does not aim to convince, coerce or convert others through bloodshed.

A GROWING PLACE ON THE INTERNATIONAL SCENE

His pontificate also had eminently political consequences, marked by a high degree of commitment on his part. A polyglot (he spoke seven languages in addition to his mother tongue), he allowed himself to genuinely become close to the people he spoke to, often going without official translators. Taking the opposite approach to Pope Pius XII, whose hesitations and delays to act against Nazism and fascism were highly controversial, John Paul II took a stand against all forms of totalitarianism. In particular, he crusaded against communism, having experienced at first hand the harm it did in Eastern Europe in his native Poland. He reduced the papacy's diplomatic contact with and signs of support for communist regimes, and played a significant part in their downfall. Conversely, he did not encourage populist revolutions in Latin America, in countries subject to strong-arm dictatorships with large Catholic majorities.

SUMMARY

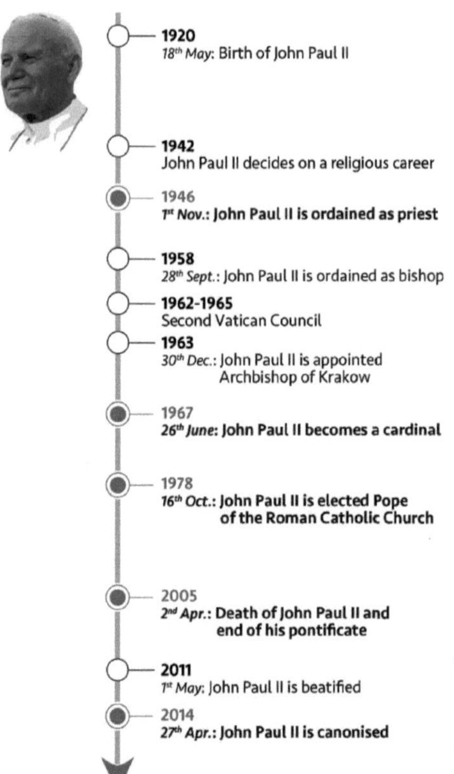

- Karol Wojtyła was appointed a bishop in Poland at the age of 38 and Archbishop of Krakow in 1963 at the Second Vatican Council. After the sudden death of Pope John Paul I in 1978, and against all predictions, he was elected

Pope of the Catholic Church on 16 October 1978 at the age of 58, and took the name John Paul II.

- As the first Slavic pope in history, and hailing from a Communist Bloc country, John Paul II was not a typical pope. A great communicator, he developed a universal pastoral approach in the course of his 104 journeys around the world, visiting 129 countries in total. He did not hesitate to address young people by launching World Youth Day in 1986.
- He supported dialogue between different religions, and took the innovative step of bringing together almost 200 religious leaders and representatives at Assisi in 1986 for a worldwide day of prayer for peace. He also began to show repentance, solemnly asking for forgiveness for the wrongs committed by Catholics towards other religions throughout history.
- He defended the principles of traditional morality, but opposed contraception, abortion and the marriage of priests, which sparked a number of fierce controversies.
- He was an ardent defender of human rights, and in his role as head of state undertook sustained diplomatic activity. He opposed totalitarian regimes in Latin America and increasingly interceded with the governments in communist countries, in this way playing a part in the end of the Eastern Bloc regimes and the fall of the Berlin Wall in 1989.
- He died in 2005, after a pontificate which had lasted more than 26 years and made a considerable impact on the history of the 20th century. He was beatified in 2011 and canonised in 2014, making him a saint of the Catholic Church.

We want to hear from you!
Leave a comment on your online library
and share your favourite books on social media!

FURTHER READING

BIBLIOGRAPHY

- Dunglas, D. (2006) *Jean-Paul II. 1920-2005*. Monaco: Éditions du Rocher.
- Dziwisz, S. (2008) *A Life with Karol: My Forty-Year Friendship with the Man Who Became Pope*. New York: Doubleday.
- Église Catholique en France (no date) *Biographie de Karol Wojtyla, pape Jean-Paul II*. [Online]. [Accessed 12 January 2017]. Available from: <http://www.eglise.catholique. fr/vatican/les-papes-recents/beatification-de-jean-paul-ii/370704-biographie-de-karol-wojtylapape-jean-paul-ii/>
- Frossard, A. and Pope John Paul II (1985) *Be Not Afraid: Pope John Paul II Speaks Out on His Life, His Beliefs, and His Inspiring Vision for Humanity*. New York: Doubleday.
- Larousse (no date) *Jean-Paul II*. [Online]. [Accessed 12 January 2017]. Available from: <http://www.larousse. fr/encyclopedie/personnage/Jean-Paul_II/125809>
- Lecomte, B. (1983) *Jean-Paul II*. Paris: Gallimard.
- The Holy See (1978) *Homily of His Holiness John Paul II for the Inauguration of his Pontificate*. [Online]. [Accessed 12 January 2017]. Available from: <https://w2.vatican. va/content/john-paul-ii/en/homilies/1978/documents/ hf_jp-ii_hom_19781022_inizio-pontificato.html>
- Vircondelet, A. (2004) *Jean-Paul II. La vie de Karol Wojtyła*. Paris: Gallimard.

ADDITIONAL SOURCES

- Cornwell, J. (2005) *The Pope in Winter: The Dark Face of John Paul II's Legacy*. London: Penguin.
- North, W. (2013) *The Life and Legacy of Pope John Paul II*. Boston, Massachusetts: Wyatt North Publishing, LLC.
- Pope John Paul II (2005) *Memory and Identity: Personal Reflections*. London: Weidenfeld & Nicolson.
- Sherwin, B.L. and Kasimow, H. (2005) *John Paul II and Interreligious Dialogue*. Eugene, Oregon: Wipf and Stock Publishers.

ICONOGRAPHIC SOURCES

- Portrait of John Paul II. Royalty-free reproduction picture.
- Catholics witness the beatification of John Paul II in Vatican City. Royalty-free reproduction picture.
- John Paul II visiting Poland in 1979. Royalty-free reproduction picture.
- John Paul II visiting New York in 1979, photograph taken by J. O'Halloran. Royalty-free reproduction picture.
- John Paul II visiting the Great Mosque of Damascus. Royalty-free reproduction picture.
- John Paul II visiting Gabon in 1983. Royalty-free reproduction picture.

DOCUMENTARIES

- *Liberating a Continent: John Paul II and the Fall of Communism*. (2016) [Documentary]. David Naglieri. Dir.

USA.

COMMEMORATIVE STATUES

- John Paul II, statue in bronze by the Italian sculptor Oliviero Rainaldi, Rome, May 2011-November 2012.
- John Paul II, statue in stone by the Polish sculptor Leszek Łysoń, Częstochowa (Poland), April 2013.
- John Paul II, statue in bronze by the Georgian-Russian sculptor Zurab Tsereteli, Square Jean XIII, Notre Dame Cathedral, Paris, October 2014.